PRUNINGS

Also by Helen Moffett:

Strange Fruit (Modjaji Books, 2009)

PRUNINGS

poems by

HELEN MOFFETT

UHLANGA

2016

Prunings
© Helen Moffett, 2016, all rights reserved

Published in Cape Town, South Africa by uHlanga in 2016
uhlangapress.co.za

Distributed outside South Africa by African Books Collective
africanbookscollective.com

ISBN: 978-0-620-72299-5

Cover illustration by Ellaphie Ward-Hilhorst

The body text of this book is set in
Goudy Retrospective 10.5pt on 15pt

෮

Grateful acknowledgement to the following publications
in which versions of the following poems were first published:
"First rain" and "Birds in Trinidad" in *Carapace*; "For a woman who
befriended me after she died", "St. Patrick's, Bridgetown",
and "Missive" (published as "Past life") in *Incwadi.*

ACKNOWLEDGEMENTS

There is a story attached to the cover art. My father, Prof Rodney Moffett, is a botanist, and the botanical artist Ellaphie Ward-Hilhorst (1920–1994) illustrated his publications. The image on the cover is taken from an unfinished, unsigned painting she did of *Rhus erosa*, one of the plants my father studied. After Ellaphie's death, John Rourke of the National Botanical Institute kindly gave my father the incomplete painting. It is used here with his permission, and as a small commemoration of the exquisite work she did for my father and others over many years.

I will always be grateful to Gus Ferguson for encouraging and publishing me in my poetic infancy; to Colleen Higgs for teaching me to find the poem within a poem; to Rustum Kozain, my first poetry editor; and to Rethabile Masilo for the enthusiasm with which he provided a cover shout.

The poems here refer to some of my travels. It would take pages to thank everyone involved, so this abbreviated list instead. Cory Kratz and the late Ivan Karp of The Center for the Study of Public Scholarship got me to Emory University in the USA. From there, Kelly McBride and the Poynter Institute got me to Florida, Chris Lee got me to Stanford (and thus to Point Reyes), and Rhoda Reddock got me to the University of the West Indies (the St. Augustine and Cave Hill campuses). I went to the Caribbean partly as a valediction to Bob Woolmer, who had recently lost his life there, a journey I couldn't have made without the support of Tim Noakes and Tom Eaton. However, the real moving force behind both my Caribbean and Indian trips was Elinor Sisulu, my much loved "magic carpet" friend. She was also responsible for the extraordinary opportunity referred to in "The visit".

I have worked with some of the finest editors in the country. But Nick Mulgrew is The One, and I hope he has a glimmering of how grateful and excited I am to have had the opportunity to pass my chaff through his sieve, and to be published by an independent press as fresh and dynamic as uHlanga. The order of the poems is his, as are some of the titles, and also the line "The kittens are children of summer", which opens "First rain".

A few of my poems refer to those who have died, sometimes cruelly young. Once again, these small commemorations are offered with respect.

—H.M.

for Nick

CONTENTS

[no. It's a failure.
I keep on in the hope that one day
I'll figure out how to write this.]

BARBADOS

A rum-shop in the north
open to the trades on three sides;
a wiry man, not young, in a red cap
shinned up a coconut tree,
brought down two, whacked open
their whiskers with a machete,
pushed a glass towards me, smiling, no fuss.

The contents: not nectar, not sweet, not cold –
the cloudy draught tasted pale-green,
like the cane-fields, the sea over the reef.

Drinking coconut water in
a rum-shop in the north,
talking cricket, liming.
This happened. We were there.

St. Patrick's, Bridgetown

Mass at seven a.m. (later is too hot),
the stone church whirring with fans,
the casual birds clapping their wings
as they coast from pillar to post,
settling for the Gospel and sermon.

This is no little England:
the stained glass suggestive
of luminous sea, sudden dawns and dusks.
The velvet priest has a voice as warm
as the air, soft, pressing on skin.

Old ladies in hats, faces seamed as toffees,
amble from bosom to bosom
to offer the sign of peace.

Arrived at this unexpected and faraway place
via an exile of sorts, an unprecedented loss:
at last, grief has room to breathe.

BIRDS IN TRINIDAD

Strange to see so familiar a shape
dressed in crimson,
rowing across a tropical sky in
dazzling dozens, a kite-tail
of fluorescent coral silk,
trailing in to roost on a viridian island,
turning to blobs of sealing wax.
It's giddying to watch,
but something is missing –
these flamboyant cousins are silent.
No clarion carks cut through
the dense air, travel across the
water to the blurry Venezuelan coast.
I'm glad I've seen the scarlet ibis,
but I'll settle for my gun-metal
country-bird, so ugly and loud.

Everglades

Norman Rockwell is dead in Florida.
Every scenic route marked
in my twelve-year-old map book
now golf estates, antacid condos,
bulldozers scraping treacle from the weeping earth,
strip malls unspooling under the greasy sun.

I drove a thousand miles to find Florida
in fragments: alligator eye, panther-proof fence,
epiphytes sucking the soupy air,
swollen-boled trees, tangling vine,
moss simmering, wet pink prairie –
Orion leaning heavily in the sky.

Point Reyes

At the visitor's centre, the seismograph
traces the humours of gigantic plates below,
pushing the thin line of ink across
unspooling paper in infinitesimally tiny, patient jags.
Without warning, it galvanizes, scribbles an angry knot.
Outside, all is sylvan peace;
underneath, the deep buzzing of bees.

KLEINMOND IN SUMMER

I   Every colour so bright
it blares. Mountains shoulder brassily
up against the butane sky.
Light reverberating with cicadas.

II   The denim sea, crimped.
Mountains float on it,
insubstantial, leached of colour,
leaning towards luminous.

III   Wind gone to bed,
water streaked with snail-trails.
Fading mountains exhale,
letting go the heat of day.

WATERFRONT

Evening

Sundown in Cape Town is not spectacular.
The mountain with six-o'-clock shadow,
the colour draining out of the bowl of the sky,
the horizon sinking in shades of dove-breast.
The distant mountains exchange texture for outline,
pastels found only in fairy tales.

Morning

Sky rinsed clear, growing blue,
the mountain a grizzled dazzle,
flaunting every groove and fissure.
The faraway mountains still airy shadows
barely darker than the egg-shell sky,
ring-a-rosy round the cranes, the masts.

Kalk Bay, April

Morning has glossed the bay with lemon oil.
The meniscus holds the swell
perpendicular to the horizon, never spilling
over the railway line in angry froth:
that belongs to winter.

The Southern Cross is following me around.
The new moon in the Cedarberg lays it out
on the chiffon scarf of the Milky Way,
in turn glitter-stroked across black velvet.

Days later, in Muizenberg, a friend's book
is launched on benign autumnal seas:
the Southern Cross has stripped down –
five minimal diamonds – reluctant to upstage.

[I don't want to include this, but
There might be something redeeming in it.]

RED ALERT

Eden hour at Nature's Valley,
iridescent dawn.
I crest a dune, to see waves charging
the silent, sliding lagoon:
smoke and froth reaching to engulf
the rippling mercury.

The vista is as flawless as
the twist of mist rising from the river,
the grand and guttural roaring of the sea –

But my nostrils twitch:
there's something out there.

Then I spot the possible predator:
alone, ~~but no less a threat for that~~
as he plods along the beach.

~~One human male.~~

I abandon the glory.
I have no choice.

Imperial Court

Remembering, reconstructing
an airy white space in the crumbling part
of Muizenburg; the white noise of surf,
the snatch of blue from the balcony,
air all around, smelling of sea.

All that light on a friend's altar:
the leaved shutters opening to reveal
a spider's calligraphy in gold and black
ordering the principles, naming the
words that keep the universe spinning.

Dozing on the sofa, I once woke
to the hum of chanting,
what I deemed as prayers.
What deity, if any, didn't matter as much
as the sense of rocking in a cradle of words.

THE BLIND WOMAN TOUCHES THE TIP OF THE ELEPHANT'S TRUNK

I   ~~It is not possible to write about the Taj Mahal.~~
~~Instead, this prefatory list:~~
Mosquitoes and touts buzzing in the pre-dawn queue,
the miasma of a drain somewhere,
the dainty female soldier briskly frisking us.
Flagstones still cool,
walkways and lawns and cloisters,
a gate, and then a second arch:
and through it, gathering light,
the sight that buckles the knees.

II   The young man at the lights
is flogging books – pirated Dan Brown
and *The Secret* on one arm;
Vikram, Salman and Vikas
on the other: he's read them all.

III   A kurta covers all the tender skin
otherwise fretted by sun and heat.
Drawstring pants don't clutch and rub
elastic rashes around your waist.
A hat will mark you as farangi
and your hair will stick out in spikes.
Wear a light shawl. It covers the head
and veils the face when necessary,
siphons out dust and insects.

Anoint the edge with sandalwood oil
against more pungent smells,
and it will remind you: you are in a place
older, more holy than you'll ever grasp.

IV   Don't bother with meat:
no pork for Muslims,
Hindus won't chew on cows,
the sheep are tough, the chickens skinny –
and inland, fish is a lottery.
Recognise that each vegetable
is considered worthy of a thousand dishes;
that no two bowls of dhal
will ever be the same.
The spices sing,
placate the bugs in your gut.
Chai and lassi will keep your skin soft,
your eyes moist and shining.
Learn to eat with your right hand.
Food tastes better this way,
and your fingers will grow gold-tipped.

VI   Ten minutes on the Grand Trunk highway,
and you can be guaranteed of seeing:
five lanes crammed into two,
hand-barrows full of melons,

three-wheeler tuk-tuks ferrying dozens,
entire families on bicycles,
sleek bullying four-by-fours,
buses held together by tinsel,
trucks dating from the Raj,
carts pulled by everything from mules to camels,
cows luxuriating in mud,
motorbikes bearing side-saddle saried women;
road signs reading "HELMET OR HALO? YOUR CHOICE".

VI I walk the length of Janpath
more than once, trailing
rickshaws, small chatty boys,
taxi-drivers promising aircon.
I walk and I walk, into a moment
of symmetry: Lutyens' Parliament on my right,
India Gate on my left;
women in cellophane colours,
men sauntering, children boisterous
as the air cools.
Sunset not a spectacle, but a long moment
of hazed sky – exactly one shade lighter than
the pink sandstone that empires left behind.

VII The most beautiful things
I saw in India
were mausoleums.

VIII   We are escorted to a shop filled with fabrics
to pay our tourist dues. We are offered tea,
and I admire the cups, delicate and filigreed.
When the parcels are wrapped into a bale
of silk and cotton and scent and colour,
our cups are swaddled, and packed up too.

IX   Returning the gaze:
the bold onyx eye
of a sacred cow
as she stuck her head
into my rickshaw.

X   I keep the cheap bag they pressed on me
in the carpet shop.
In it, a last hoard of Sikkim tea,
incense, cardamom.

When I have doubts like vertigo –
Was I there? Was it real? –
I open it and inhale:
the yelling shades
come back to me.

O.R.T.

The shock is dreadful:
Who are all these ugly people?
Why are their clothes so drab?
Who stole the colours from my eye?

MISSIVE

Your hair needs a cut,
though it's thinning now;
looking down from a balcony and
spotting you unexpectedly,
I see the tender swirl
of scalp emerging at your summit;
and am plunged back onto a bed,
drowning in your hair as it pours down
on either side of my face, your
fingers pushing it away
from my mouth.

Your hair was longer than mine then.
It will never come back.

Ex-lover

~~It's about time I wrote you a poem;~~
~~everyone else has one.~~

COMFORTER

Cataloging the times you gave me solace:
Four deaths, one near-miss.
Three cancer scares,
holding my hand at the gynaecologist's,
clinking glasses
when the scans came back clear.
The day I recounted
wrecking my career with a whistle.
But most: erasing the fourteen frozen years,
empty belly swelling only with fat,
breasts that were dead weight –
until I nourished you.

THE WOMAN WHO ASKED FOR GLASSES FOR HER BIRTHDAY, OR, HALF-FULL

for Karina

She has dozens of them in sets, glittering
ranks in break-front cabinets.
But now she wants single glasses
from our own cupboards and pantries.
She wants to place her lips
where we sip at the ~~half-empty,~~
~~half-full~~ globes that hold the dregs of our lives,
the flowering of scent and bubbles
on the tongue; the plain tap we gulp,
not caring about chlorine tang:
all held entire in these brittle vessels
until the crack, the smash, the
fragments to be swept up before they
cut our soles to ribbons.

But she wants the glasses that have survived.
They might break tomorrow –
for now, they quench our drought.

First rain

for Gus

The kittens are children of summer,
but now the whole world shines like abalone,
and brick has a new slick, causing
hesitation, shaking of paws.
The smells are fresh, intriguing –
and here is something else brand-new:
a snail, inching up a wall. Meg stretches
into an tentative stripe to investigate
the nacreous interloper. Friend? Foe?
Something to eat? A little paw dabs,
and the snail becomes a barnacle.
Baffled, Meg retreats into her shell.

WISDOM

for Antjie Krog

I'm inclined to trust her,
this woman with a child's clear vision,
who points out the scabrous sores
on the Emperor's bare bum,
and sees magic in unpropitious dust.

We discuss stars,
the Seven Sisters;
Pleiades in Western lore,
but in African skies, an earthier tale –
a sign of harvest, soil, seed and dung:
a marker for this country,
slung between pit latrines and constellations,
rooted in both elements – of shit and stars.

Christmas Eve, Mouille Point, 2004

Coming in from catching this morning's
dolphins on a tourmaline sea full of inscapes,
carrying our kayaks up the beach, I
catch something else in the corner of my eye:
a woman washing her feet at the beach tap.

All the time we're stowing paddles and
divesting ourselves of life-vests,
she's there, teetering her way
through a clumsy pavanne of hygiene:
I realise she's washing her entire body,

piece by modest piece,
under her loose and faded shift.
She shifts her bulk on small feet,
almost as broad as they're long:
tell-tale sign of a bare-foot life.

Looking more closely, I spot
further accoutrements of her toilet –
A rectangle of pink soap, striated
with white: the kind used for
scrubbing stoeps when I was a child.

(Also, a sleek bottle of Pantene.)

This woman, to whom
ten much-vaunted years
have brought precisely this much:

a public tap on an old whites-only beach.

For Sophie, a crumb of comfort

Fourteen and fifteen were my worst years,
all at once acutely self-aware,
each movement phosphorescent –
but still invisible, except for the unwanted
glances checking new height and breasts.
Emphatically no longer a child, bored
with childish things – but still
an immeasurable distance from adulthood:
too young to be nostalgic, yet seized
by wild and terrible yearning triggered by
snatches of music and changes in the weather –
desperately wanting understanding, but
snapping at everyone who asked
"What's the matter?"

All I can tell you is that it passes.
Sunnier realms are at hand,
and the whole time, life will slip by
~~(you will know in the end)~~ too fast.

leaking light from the sky in my eye.

BIRTHDAY IN THE BO-KAAP

for Tatamkhulu Afrika

We celebrated a birthday today.
Geoffrey read a poem about a death-day,
a reminder of the grave that will cradle us all;
then we were served samoosas, cake and tea.

I also have a Tatamkhulu tale to tell:
I published one of his poems,
and he refused to take money for it.
But one day the receptionist at OUP
appeared flustered in my office:
"There's a Mister Afrika for you
at the front desk. *He looks like, er, a bergie.*"
Intrigued, I went to investigate: and met
a cricket of a man, all sinew and beard;
truth be told, he did smell rather ripe.
His face a twist of tallow lit from within,
his manner flirtatious in the courtly way
of a man aged beyond expectations of response.
He'd come to buy a book.
I begged him to accept one free:
he was obdurate, adamant.
He had the money; he wanted to pay.

"My poems are not for sale; but literary prizes –
Hah! I'll take those cheques anyday."
It's a little-known fact that a publisher's
is the least convenient place to purchase
one's reading matter, but his book emerged,
neatly wrapped, at last.
We weren't out of the woods yet, though:
I'd placed the order, so the price was
automatically discounted by a third.
He shook a biltonged finger:
"I suspect some crookery here:
You're all very naughty – but kind!"

One place he still breathes and carps
and chuckles and hoots is on the pages
of his increasingly rarely-spotted books.
His poems remain my friends. Mown,
he is free of his failing flesh now.
Now the stars he collected in his haversack
fly swooping and singing around his soul.

Thief

for Steve de Gruchy

What the river seizes,
it holds.

THE VISIT

after editing In Our Lifetime: The biography of
Walter and Albertina Sisulu, *by Elinor Sisulu*

The day after the book launch,
I am invited to the Sisulu home:
Walter wants to thank me in person.
On arrival, Albertina's sprightly hug
cannot diminish my awe.
I am ushered into the presence
of the icon, an old man in a wheelchair.
First, a short homily to the assembled family:
"You see, if you want something done well,
you must ask a woman to do it!"
Then he gestures me closer, reaches
for my hand. I kneel at his slippered feet.
He proceeds with a formal speech
of thanks and praise, as if the honour
were not all mine.
As he winds up, he peers into my face,
now streaming with foolish tears:
"I know you," he says. "I *know* you.
From where do I know you?"

It turns out his prodigious memory
has retrieved my face from a breakfast
twelve years ago, during the first
talks between the ANC
and the then-regime; time long gone.

He was kind, fatherly to me then;
now his gift for connection spans the years
as it bridged bitter divides, catastrophic clefts –
incarceration, a family scattered by wolves.
Nothing has dented, tainted his smile;
dry fingers trembling in my clasp,
his gaze, agate with age, seeing me clearly.
And feeling the force of that,
I want to bawl into his lap.
Instead I sit back,
blow my nose, accept biscuits and tea.
The rest of the visit, I hold his cup for him
as we watch a cricket match on TV.

FOR A WOMAN WHO BEFRIENDED ME AFTER SHE DIED
[NEEDS NEW TITLE?]

in memory of Liesl Abrahams Steyn

Tall candle of a woman,
dark nimbus of hair around
a face like a flame:
four weeks after your festive nuptials
("the happiest day of my life," you said)
a dam burst in your beautiful head.
You died in your husband's arms,
for which crumb of mercy we were thankful.
The wedding guests regathered, ashen,
our dancing shoes now following your coffin.

It was only after your death
I really came to know you: arm's length in life,
you came closer, whispering in my ear:
"Write thank-you notes at once."
"Double the quantity of chocolate in recipes."
"Lightning can strike at any time."
"Have a day to remember."
"Love is worth the risk."

Those who loved, still love you,
locked their fingers together
and stumbled on:
now you are the one left behind –
nothing so ruthless, merciful
as the passage of time.

But still I hear snatches of your voice:
"Don't let your fear of the water
stop you from learning to swim."

THERAPY

My shrink sent me sea-kayaking,
divining that what I most needed
was space untrammeled by fear
of anything human. The monsters
of the deep held no terrors.
Loosed from caution's leash,
no need to look over my shoulder,
salt splash, sun-gilt in my face,
the swinging swell of the sea
revived another self in me:
a little girl, alone, on a pony
cresting the burning waves of the Karoo.

SALVAGE

~~What do other people do~~
~~when they're in dreadful pain?~~
~~Not the kind that requires morphine;~~
~~but the sort for which there is no cure~~
~~except time; and that's never any good~~
~~at the time.~~
~~I remember a bereft friend~~
~~moving from room to room,~~
~~indoors to outside, sitting, then standing,~~
~~pacing, up the stairs and down,~~
~~hoping the brute dog might lag~~
~~momentarily behind. No such luck.~~

~~I'm leafing through options, like dealing~~
~~a pack of cards; so far, I've tried music~~
~~(baroque – they say it calms the brain),~~
~~housework, filing, cups of tea.~~
~~I keep hoping to find a pattern, a key~~
~~that will either switch the misery off~~
~~or make sense of it, give it some grand shape.~~
This wretchedness so unaesthetic.
~~Pathetic.~~

~~My mind now matches my office:~~
~~paperwork strewn everywhere.~~
~~It's a mess. And it has to be sorted out.~~

Pain is like provisional tax:
it's not just that there's no escaping paying;
it's the onerous, inexorable chore
of keeping account, ~~nitpicking,~~ calculating costs,
a reckoning demanding my full attention,
no matter how I shuffle the paper.

glory   glory   glory

Voices in the head

~~I have no intention of acting on~~
~~these sulphuric whispers.~~

Twitching

This cell has become an aviary:
strange and speckled feathers
whirl and drift and float.
I try to feed with seeds,
this motley multitude,
keeping me company
keeping me.

[hmm, no.]

POETRY FOR THE PEOPLE

ɞ

ALSO AVAILABLE:

Questions for the Sea by **Stephen Symons**

Failing Maths and My Other Crimes by **Thabo Jijana**
WINNER OF THE 2016 INGRID JONKER PRIZE FOR POETRY

Matric Rage by **Genna Gardini**
COMMENDED FOR THE 2016 INGRID JONKER PRIZE FOR POETRY

the myth of this is that we're all in this together by **Nick Mulgrew**

ɞ

AVAILABLE FROM GOOD BOOKSTORES IN SOUTH AFRICA
& ELSEWHERE FROM THE AFRICAN BOOKS COLLECTIVE,
IN PRINT AND DIGITAL

ɞ

UHLANGAPRESS.CO.ZA

Printed in the United States
By Bookmasters